01341 109 75452

2000
12:00

Rough Guides

25 Ultimate experiences

Ethical Travel

Make the most of your time on Earth

280101

ROUGH GUIDES

25 YEARS 1982–2007

NEW YORK • LONDON • DELHI

Contents

Introduction

EXPERIENCES have always been at the heart of the Rough Guide concept. A group of us began writing the books **25 years ago** (hence this celebratory mini series) and wanted to share the kind of travels we had been doing ourselves. It seems bizarre to recall that in the early 1980s, travel was very much a minority pursuit. Sure, there was a lot of tourism around, and that was reflected in the guidebooks in print, which traipsed around the established sights with scarcely a backward look at the local population and their life. We wanted to change all that: to put a country or a city's popular culture centre stage, to highlight the clubs where you could hear local music, drink with people you hadn't come on holiday with, watch the local football, join in with the festivals. And of course we wanted to push travel a bit further, inspire readers with the confidence and knowledge to break away from established routes, to find pleasure and excitement in remote islands, or desert routes, or mountain treks, or in street culture.

Twenty-five years on, that thinking seems pretty obvious: we all want to experience something real about a destination, and to seek out travel's **ultimate experiences**. Which is exactly where these **25 books** come in. They are not in any sense a new series of guidebooks. We're happy with the series that we already have in print. Instead, the **25s** are a collection of ideas, enthusiasms and inspirations: a selection of the very best things to see or do – and not just before you die, but now. Each selection is gold dust. That's the brief to our writers: there is no room here for the average, no space fillers. Pick any one of our selections and you will enrich your travelling life.

But first of all, take the time to browse. Grab a half dozen of these books and let the ideas percolate … and then begin making your plans.

Mark Ellingham
Founder & Series Editor, Rough Guides

Ultimate
experiences
Ethical
Travel

Digging
AND
dancing

IN MADAGASCAR

01

As someone who'd never wielded a shovel in her life, I was pretty pleased with my first day's efforts on the Azafady Pioneer programme. Azafady makes a point of pitching its volunteers into the thick of things, which in my case meant digging a well in a remote Madagascan village, bounded on one side by forested hillsides and on the other by the most idyllic beaches I'd ever set eyes on. Not that we had much chance to gaze at the scenery. Half buried in red dust and mud, most of the day was spent digging and slapping on trowels of cement under the watchful eye of our local project coordinator.

Sometimes, volunteering initiatives seem geared more towards benefiting the volunteers themselves than the communities they are there ostensibly to help. But this isn't the case with Azafady, where the work carried out – supporting NGOs on a range of health, sanitation and environmental schemes – really does make a positive impact on the environment and lives of local people. It's an award-winning scheme that provides a very special way to get under the surface of life on La Grande Île. Moreover, all the profits are ploughed back into sustainable development.

After an intensive seven-day orientation course, where you're taught the basics of local Malagasi dialects, the volunteer work proper begins. Ours involved planting fruit trees, making puppets and writing songs to help teach children about the importance of washing their hands before eating. Out in the forest, we spent days collecting rare seeds, surveying the impact of logging and assisting with studies of birds, plants and lemurs.

The hands-on nature of the work means it can be physically demanding at times; but Azafady make sure there's enough downtime for its volunteers to surf and, more importantly, hang out with the local people they work with. There were some amazing parties on the beach outside Ambinanibe, the village where we dug the well. Fuelled by bottles of warm Three Horses beer, we were shown how to drum, sing bawdy songs in the local lingo and, best of all, do the *mangaliba* – the sexiest dance in all the Indian Ocean.

need to know

Volunteers on **Azafady's** ten-week **Pioneer programme** are required to raise a minimum donation of £2000 ($3900), with all funds sent to the projects in Madagascar. Flights cost extra. For more, log on to Ⓦwww. azafady.org.

Himalayan homestay,
KUMAON 02

As one of the holiest Hindu pilgrimage sites in the Indian Himalaya, Baijnath is busy year round, but over the festival of Makar Sankranti, in mid-January, all hell breaks loose when villagers from the surrounding valleys pour in to town for the famous annual livestock fair. Most desirable among the animals traded on the muddy market ground here are the ponies brought in by the nomadic Bhotiyas, who pasture them on the grasslands of the Tibetan Plateau before leading them down to market in the winter.

The names, uses and cost of other exotic merchandise – borax, musk pods, dried apricots and salt horns – are explained to me by my companions from the village of Sonargaon, a few hours' bus ride further north into the mountains. I've been staying with a family for a month as part of a grassroots volunteer program called ROSE (Rural Organization for Social Elevation), and this trip to the bright lights of the Makar Sankranti fair has been one of its highlights.

ROSE was set up as a development initiative to alleviate some of the hardships of rural life in the Kumaon region, where around 75 percent of people are landless farmers. Paying guests of the scheme get to work on a range of community-inspired projects that funds raised by them beforehand – along with bed-and-board money – help to pay for. During my stay I lent a hand to digging new latrines, planting trees and delivering smokeless, wood-free stoves to de-forested villages. I also helped out with daily chores in the fields and at home: feeding the cattle, planting barley and potatoes, and fixing roofs ahead of the summer rains.

Working alongside your hosts in this way leaves a vivid sense of how such small improvements might really make a real difference. But the stay wasn't all toil. At the end, the eldest son from my host family arranged for a team of porters to trek with us further north into the mountains, to the snout of the Pinadri Glacier, overlooked by some of the highest peaks in the entire Indian Himalaya.

need to know

Other than for the festival, the best time to visit Kumaon is in early spring (March–April) and late summer (Sept–Oct). Stays organized by ROSE typically cost around Rs350 (£4.10/$7.75) per night; and there's also a one-off registration fee of Rs3500 (£41/$77.75). For more info, go to ⓦwww.rosekanda.info.

03 COUNTING dolphins
in the Med

Need to know

Earthwatch (Ⓦwww.earthwatch
.org) recruits and supplies
volunteers to established
conservation projects around
the world, from lions in Kenya
to glaciers in Alaska. "Spanish
Dolphins" – one of 140 projects
supported by the charity – lasts
twelve days and costs from £995
($1950) depending on season.

"Sighting!" shouts Captain Ricardo Sagarminaga, as the dorsal fins flicker into view. Moments later, a hundred striped dolphins are speeding alongside the boat, leaping out of the waves and riding the wake of the bow. On board Toftevaag, our antique wooden sailboat, a very international crew of volunteers and scientists springs into action. The Dane grabs the sonar reader, the American opens the behaviour log, the Spaniard sets up her SLR, and the Brit slaps on the factor 40. It's going to be a long, hot afternoon of serious dolphin counting.

The volunteers, mostly office workers in need of some sea air, have set sail off the southern coast of Spain with the international environmental charity, Earthwatch, to play at being marine biologists for a dozen days. On board, we help scientists to monitor dolphin populations, pollution levels and the impact of over-fishing. Photo-identifications, behavioural notes, skin swabs, environmental data and oceanographic readings are all gathered during the frequent sightings, and are transformed into impressive graphs and reports by the captain's wife, marine biologist Dr. Ana Cañadas. In 2000, Ana and Ricardo's research into a decline in dolphin populations persuaded the Spanish government to create a Marine Protected Area in this region. Today, the couple continue to monitor and manage the area, working alongside visiting scientists, Earthwatch volunteers and local fishing communities.

For us volunteers, working on the boat is no easy ride – assisting the scientists during sightings, cooking and cleaning for the whole crew – in a sweltering galley – sleeping onboard in cramped bunks and setting sail at 7am. But awe-inspiring encounters are practically guaranteed. Common, bottlenose and striped dolphins, pilot whales, sperm whales and loggerhead turtles are all regularly sighted from the boat, and we leave the Toftevaag with a greater understanding of marine conservation issues, and with memories of wild dolphins leaping from the open sea.

04

IL NGWESI: SUSTAINABLE
SAFARIS WITH THE
Maasai

North of Mount
Kenya, the Laikipia
region, a vast sweep
of rangelands, ridges and seasonal rivers, stretches out
towards the northern deserts. Here, former ranches
are converting to eco-tourism and conservation,
and pastoral communities are setting up innovative
experiments in tourist development.

Many places in Laikipia make efforts to limit their environmental footprint and Il Ngwesi – owned and run by the six-thousand-strong Il Ngwesi Laikipiak Maasai community – has taken the lead.

The lodge, located on a remote, bush-covered ridge, is delightful. It's a bird-watcher's paradise: you awake to a jaw-dropping dawn chorus, and birds – from drongos to hornbills – fill the air all day long, crowding the footpaths and branches, and often appearing in the rooms themselves. Six huge *bandas* (artfully rustic, thatch and tree-trunk cottages) are spaced out along the west-facing slope, their open-sided fronts graced with magnificent decks and chunky furniture made of polished branches. *Banda* number one has almost embarrassingly good views of the elephants that congregate around Il Ngwesi's magical waterhole, and, like number five, features a giant mosquito-netted four-poster bed that you can pull out onto the deck.

There's no wood burning or fossil fuel use at Il Ngwesi – all electricity is supplied by solar power – and the community has a water-use association to monitor consumption and pollution, ensuring the local herds have plenty to drink and leaving enough over for the lodge's beautiful infinity pool. Although strictly a private conservancy, the area swarms with wildlife, and game walks, with Maasai guides and armed rangers, are the norm. It's especially satisfying that all the money goes back into the community, which – among other things – has enabled them to bring back rhinos, formerly hunted out of the area, and to track and monitor at least one pack of highly endangered African wild dogs.

need to know

Il Ngwesi is approximately 1hr 30min rough drive from the nearest road. *Bandas* cost around £260/$500 per person per night based on two sharing, including all meals (Ⓦwww.lets-go-travel.net). You can also book the whole lodge on a self-catering basis: bring your own food, and the kitchen staff will cook it for you.

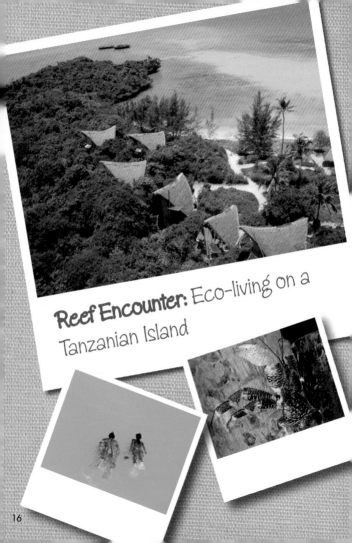

Reef Encounter: Eco-living on a Tanzanian Island

05

It's difficult to know which way to look, snorkelling in the turquoise waters off Chumbe Island. At the oriental sweetlips, bobbing in unison around a huge coral fan? At the blue-spotted stingrays, shuffling under the sand along the bottom? Or at any one of the other four hundred or so species of fish that help make the island's reef, Tanzania's first marine protected area, one of the finest coral gardens in the world.

Overlooking the reef at Chumbe's western edge are seven palm-thatched eco-lodges; the rest of the island is a designated nature reserve of creeping mangroves and coral rag forest, left to the local wildlife – including the rare Ader's duiker and the endangered coconut crab, the largest land crab in the world. Everything about the lodges shouts "green": their roofs are designed to collect rainwater, which is then filtered before running through to the shower; hot water and electricity are provided by solar power; toilets are of the composting variety; and the air-conditioning system is probably the most efficient you'll ever see – a pulley lowers the bedroom's tree-top front wall, cooling the room with a fresh sea breeze.

With a maximum of twelve guests at any one time, Chumbe is a real honeymoon hideaway – indeed, it's often used to round off a once-in-a-lifetime safari, maybe as an ecological appeasement for all those internal flights spent whizzing from one park to another on the African mainland. The only other visitors are school children from nearby Zanzibar, who visit the island on educational snorkelling trips. Watching them come back in off the reef, chatting excitedly about following a hawksbill turtle along the outer shelf or trying to outdo each other with the size of the groupers they've just seen, is almost as much fun as drifting above the coral yourself.

need to know

Chumbe Island Eco-Lodge (@www.chumbeisland.com) is reached by boat from Zanzibar, a short flight from Dar es Salaam in Tanzania. A night in an eco-lodge costs from £80–105/$150–200 per person (including all meals, guided nature walks and snorkelling); all profits go back into the conservation of the island.

06

SNOW WONDER:

Podding it up in the Swiss Alps

You can barely see Whitepod, a zero-impact, luxury "camp" until you're almost upon it, so well is it camouflaged against the deep snows of this tranquil forest setting, high in the Alps and far from any roads.

Each pod – eight of them comprise the camp – is a mini geodesic dome sheathed in white canvas, a sturdy, igloo-shaped construction set on a raised wooden platform. But this is no wilderness campsite: the emphasis is squarely on modern, five-star comforts. Inside each pod – heated by its own wood-burning stove – you get a proper king-size bed with multiple fluffy down covers and comfortable armchairs, along with an iPod and designer toiletries.

So far, so typical of the ski industry – hardly the world's most environmentally sound, with all those snow cannon and piste-grooming machines, not to mention traffic jams on Alpine roads. But Whitepod, the idea of a Swiss entrepreneur, is different: no concrete is used in the pods, so there is no impact on the ground beneath, and everything is sourced locally, from the logs to the solar power to the organic food.

For showers, meals and relaxing with other guests, you cross to the wooden chalet in the centre of the site, which has been updated inside – all soft lighting, comfortable lounging and chic designer touches. The atmosphere is great – out in the wild woods, boasting spectacular views of the mountains, yet with every comfort taken care of in an understated, very Swiss way.

And Whitepod's impeccable credentials don't get in the way of a good time: you can indulge in all sorts of Alpine activities up here, including dog-sledding with huskies, parahiking (hike to the top of a summit and then paraglide down), horse-riding and more. This far from the resorts, the only skiing on offer is testing off-piste stuff – with the prospect of a relaxing massage and a spectacular sunset when you get back to your pod.

need to know

Whitepod is located near Villars, in southwestern Switzerland. Rates start at 325CHF (£138/$270) per pod, per night (for two guests). See @www.whitepod.com for details.

SUMMER trips to France often mean *le camping*: a couple of weeks in a high-density site amid ranks of über-equipped German RVs and the pervasive whiff of shower gel from the dreaded sanitary block. There are, however, alternatives.

One of a new breed of cooler, greener, environmentally friendlier sites, set up so you can camp without the burden of bringing your own tents, is Tipis Indiens, a tiny farm-based campsite at Gèdre, deep in the Pyrenees. Set on a glorious natural balcony at 1300m, looking straight up the valley to the jaw-dropping Cirque de Gavarnie, the site consists of four Native American tipis, well spaced and simply furnished with beds, lanterns and traditional Native American decor. Each has its own little campfire (logs provided) and an uninterrupted, chocolate-box view of the mountains, while a stone barn nearby houses a kitchen and dining room, complete with a long pine table.

Gèdre is slap in the middle of one of the most dramatic parts of the Pyrenees, perfectly placed for day walks around the green, barn-studded foothills, or more serious treks up to the watershed above Gavarnie and the wild Saugué Plateau. You can catch buses further afield to visit the grottoes at Luz Saint Saveur, Trabés and Lourdes.

In terms of your carbon footprint, this is a particularly sound holiday choice because it's one that can – if you're starting out from the UK, at least – be made without needing to get in a plane or car. Fast train services run all the way to Lourdes, from where regular buses shuttle up the valley to Gèdre. Once on site, it's possible to get around with a combination of buses, the occasional taxi, and lots of healthy, zero-carbon walking through glorious scenery.

need to know

Tipis Indiens (🌐www.tipis-indiens.com) is 42km from Lourdes, in the far south of France. A week's stay in a tipi costs £200–300 ($390–585), depending on the month.

07 COOL CAMPING
in the
French Pyrenees

Translucent turquoise water swarming with rainbow-coloured fish; sand the colour and consistency of finely ground pearls; a hinterland of irrepressible tropical greenery . . . it sounds like paradise. But for the inhabitants of this remote stretch of the Mozambique coast, still licking its wounds after four decades of civil war, life isn't a beach. Infant mortality runs at one in three, and – thanks to rampant malaria, a shortage of clean water and poor sanitation – average life expectancy struggles to exceed forty years.

It was exactly this glaring juxtaposition of beach idyll and grinding poverty that inspired a team of young British entrepreneurs to establish a tourist resort with a difference on the deserted seashore near Guludo village, just north of the Quirimbas National Park. But instead of carving out an exclusive enclave, the primary aim of the project was to provide a sustainable means of alleviating hardship in the neighbourhood: 55 local people have been trained to work in the tourist lodge, and one day they'll run the place entirely.

Guludo Beach Lodge was designed to have minimal impact on the environment. Its nine 'rooms' are thatched, tented shelters, or , with raised inner platforms – private, but open to the sea breezes and views, and equipped with luxurious beds, mozzie nets and al fresco marble bathrooms. All the wonderful food is sourced locally, and waste recycled.

Far from being screened from local conditions, guests are actively encouraged to visit Guludo village, patronize handicraft businesses there, play in the weekly locals versus staff football match, and generally get involved in the development projects financed by the resort. Five percent of the lodge's profits are channeled directly into schemes such as well excavation, health and sanitation workshops, support and training for midwives and – most ambitiously – the construction of a new school for the village.

08

Guludo Beach Lodge

need to know

Prices start at $205 (£105), rising to $255 (£130) in peak season (mid-August to early-January), when the weather is perfect for the beach. ⓦwww.bespokeexperience.com.

09 DISCOVERING *treasure*
on Jamaica's coast

In countries whose main income is from tourism, holidaying can be a somewhat surreal experience – and Jamaica is no exception. The big resorts are dominated by fenced off all-inclusive hotels, the best bits of beach are pay-to-enter and most visitors' only interaction with Jamaicans is when ordering a beer or a burger. It's easy to see why savvier tourists have begun to forego resorts entirely in favour of something more authentic, heading away from the white sand and gin-clear waters of the north to the black sand and breakers of the south.

In Treasure Beach, sustainable, community-based tourism is the order of the day. Locals have taken control of development, opening low-key hotels and guesthouses instead of selling up to the multinational chains, ensuring that the tourist dollar goes straight into the community and not some US bank account. Rather than themed restaurants and bars selling flavoured margaritas and bongs of beer, you'll find laid-back, locally run outfits where you can feast on Jamaican home-cooking, learn the art of dominoes Caribbean-style or sip a white rum while the regulars teach you the latest dancehall moves. And thanks mostly to community group BREDS – named after "*bredrin*", the patois term for friend – tourism has had a tangibly positive effect: funds raised by visitor donations and an annual triathlon and fishing tournament have, among many other achievements, bought an ambulance (essential in a place where few have a car and the nearest hospital is fifteen miles away), upgraded the local school and given financial aid to low-income families whose lives were ripped apart by Hurricane Ivan. A cheering thought as you hop in a fishing pirogue-cum-tour boat to head up the coast to Pelican Bar, a rickety shack built on a sandbar a mile out to sea – easily the coolest drinking spot in Jamaica, with not a flavoured margarita in sight.

need to know

For info on everything Treasure Beach, from accommodation to restaurants and tours, visit ⓦwww.treasurebeach.net. For more on **BREDS**, visit ⓦwww.breds.org.

CATCHING THE SEA BREEZE AT

Elsewhere

10

Few places in Asia have changed as dramatically over the past few decades as Goa. Since the advent of direct charter flights from northern Europe in the 1980s, this former Portuguese colony on India's tropical southwest coast has been struggling to keep its nose above the rising tide of concrete. It's no Costa Blanca – high-rise hotels are few and far between – but the distinctive Indo-Portuguese way of life that once prevailed here has been almost completely submerged.

Only one stretch of the white-sand beaches that extend along its coastline has escaped development. Flanked by palms and wispy casuarinas trees, the solitary colonial-era house Elsewhere rises from the dunes near the village of Mandrem, looking exactly as it did a century or more ago, when the great-grandfather of the present owner, local fashion photographer Denzil Sequeira, bought it as a hot-season retreat.

Rather than sell or lease the land behind it to a hotel chain, Denzil decided to renovate one of the derelict houses as an exclusive seaside bolt-hole – in traditional Goan style. High-pitched terracotta roofs with jackwood beams allow the sea breezes blowing through the shuttered windows to circulate – so no air-con is necessary – while the pillared veranda, painted in earthy reds and limewash, is possibly the loveliest spot on India's entire southwestern shoreline. Down on the beach, fish eagles flap lazily over the surf, and olive marine turtles nest unmolested beside traditional wooden outriggers.

A week here for a small group will cost you a lot less than it would in one of the snazzy charter complexes further south. The impact is minimal (no electricity generators, water guzzling pools or lawns) and the experience of Goa infinitely more authentic. Villagers plod past picking cashew fruit or coconuts, and Elsewhere's resident chef buys fish literally straight off the boat just after dawn.

Reclined on an antique Portuguese planter's chair, you can watch the sun setting over the Arabian Sea, secure in the knowledge that your luxury break is actually helping to protect this little corner of paradise.

need to know

Elsewhere (@www.aseascape.com) comfortably accommodates six people. A week at the house costs £546–2100 ($1000–4000) depending on the season.

11 Blazing a trail at
DANA NATURE RESERVE

When you think of eco-friendly travel, you don't immediately think of the Middle East. In environmental terms, the region is a disaster, characterized by a general lack of awareness of the issues and poor – if any – legislative safeguards. But Jordan is quietly working wonders and the impact in the last few years of the country's Royal Society for the Conservation of Nature (RSCN) has been striking: areas of outstanding natural beauty are now under legal protection and sustainable development is squarely on the political agenda.

The RSCN's flagship project is the Dana Nature Reserve, the Middle East's only successful example of sustainable tourism. Up until 1993, Dana was dying: the stone-built mountain village was crumbling, its hinterland suffering from hunting and overgrazing, while local people were abandoning their homes in search of better opportunities in the towns.

Then the RSCN stepped in and set up the Dana Nature Reserve, drawing up zoning plans to establish wilderness regions and semi-intensive use areas where tourism could be introduced, building a guesthouse and founding a scientific research station. Virtually all the jobs – tour guides, rangers, cooks, receptionists, scientists and more – were taken by villagers.

Today, over eight hundred local people benefit from the success of Dana, and the reserve's running costs are covered almost entirely from tourism revenues. The Guesthouse continues to thrive, with its spectacular views out over the V-shaped Dana valley, while a three-hour walk away in the hills lies the idyllic Rummana campsite, from where you can embark on dawn excursions to watch ibex and eagles.

But the reserve also stretches down the valley towards the Dead Sea Rift – and here, a memorable five-hour walk from the Guesthouse, stands the Feinan Wilderness Lodge, set amidst an arid sandy landscape quite different from Dana village. The lodge is powered by solar energy and lit by candles; with no road access at all, it's a bewitchingly calm and contemplative desert retreat.

need to know

Dana (ⓦwww.rscn.org.jo) lies 200km south of Amman. Double rooms at the Guesthouse (all year) or Feinan Wilderness Lodge (Sept–June) cost around £33 ($62). Rummana campsite (March–Oct) costs around £13 ($24) per person. All prices include breakfast.

12

COSTA RICA
family
adventure

THE BEST THING ABOUT a family adventure trip is that kids are up for anything "if everyone else is doing it". Which in Costa Rica means a full turn-out not just to go whitewater rafting, but for a 5am glide down the jungle waterways of Tortuguero – a huge swathe of mangrove swamps and lagoons, where howler monkeys and spider monkeys cavort in the canopy, and river otters and caiman dip into the riverbanks. In summer you can also go down to the beach at night to see green sea turtles hauling themselves up to lay their eggs on the Caribbean beach.

What kid could resist that? And who could fail to be excited by Arenal, Costa Rica's most active volcano, best observed floating on your back in a swimming pool, watching puffs of smoke emerge, like some home science kit?

From one wonder to another: the Monteverde Cloud Forest Reserve. This is the country's most famous ecosystem, where cloud rather than rain nurtures a huge diversity of wildlife, including most of the iconic tree frogs. They and indeed the cloudforest itself are under threat from climate change, but the protection of this reserve – and Costa Rica's acknowledgment of its wildlife as a national resource – is an inspiration. And the frogs, which you can see most easily in the village's well-designed Ranario, are a phenomenon, every possible colour and size, from fingernail-miniature to something as big as a rabbit.

Monteverde is also ingeniously making its forest into a resource by creating a knock-out experience for kids – canopy zipwire tours. If you think you've done zipwires, think again: these are vast, climaxing in a six-hundred-metre ride, strung out across a whole valley.

After all the action, and the travelling, you're more than ready for seaside. Which for our group meant the coastal park of Manuel Antonio – perfect white sandy Pacific beach, where we gazed up from the water to see capuchin monkeys descending on our sandwiches.

need to know

Most of the adventure holiday companies offer Costa Rica as a family trip; ours was with **Explore! Family Adventures** (ⓦ www.exploreworldwide.com).

LIFF ON THE QUIET SIDE:
Homestays on
Lake Titicaca

13

Set against a backdrop of desert mountains, the shimmering waters of Lake Titicaca have formed the heart of Peru's highland altiplano civilizations since ancient times, nourishing the Pukara, Tiawanaku and Colla peoples, whose enigmatic ruins still encrust the shoreline. More than seventy of Titicaca's scattered islands remain inhabited, among them the famous *islas flotantes*, floating islands created centuries ago by the Uros Indians from compacted reed beds.

In recent decades, such attractions have made the lake one of Peru's top visitor destinations; as a consequence, only in the most remote corners can you still encounter traditional settlements that aren't overrun with camera-toting outsiders.

Yet merely by visiting such isolated places, aren't travellers running the risk of eroding the very ways of life they've come to see? Not in distant Anapia, a cluster of five tiny islets near the border with Bolivia, whose ethnic Aymara residents – descendants of the altiplano's original inhabitants – live mainly from subsistence agriculture and fishing, maintaining their own music, dance, costume and weaving traditions.

Here, fifteen Anapian families have got together to create their own homestay scheme. Each takes it in turn to host visitors, in the same way they've traditionally rotated grazing rights. Accommodation is simple, but clean and warm: you get your own room and bathroom – sharing meals with the host family on tables spread with brightly coloured homespun cloth. Potatoes are the main staple, and if you're lucky they'll be prepared *huatia*-style, baked in an earth oven with fresh fish and herbs from the lake shore.

Walking, fishing, sailing and rowing trips fill your time. A guided excursion also takes you to the uninhabited island of Vipisque, where the Aymara rear vicuñas – small, cinnamon-coloured cousins of the alpaca, prized for their fine wool. From the hilltop at the centre of the island, the view extends all the way across Lake Titicaca to the ice peaks of Bolivia's Cordillera Real – one of South America's most magnificent panoramas.

need to know

Homestays on Anapia can be arranged on spec at the jetty in Pumo, a two-hour boat ride from the island, or as part of a package offered by operators such as **Insider Tours** (Ⓦwww.insider-tours.com).

14 Meet the People: CUBA

With his sticking-out ears and Groucho Marx moustache, Lucio Parada Camenate makes an unlikely revolutionary hero, but as the face of Fruit Passion, his mugshot appears on juice cartons across the world, wherever Fair Trade products are marketed – much to the evident amusement of his colleagues, who tease him mercilessly for being *famoso*.

Lucio is one of several guest-star guides featured on Fair Trade's "Meet the People" tour of Cuba – part holiday, part crash course on the culture and society of Fidel Castro's economically disadvantaged island. Visiting coffee plantations, citrus orchards and juice factories – not to mention primary schools and maternity wards – may not sound as alluring as slurping mojitos by the poolside in Fuertaventura, but the reality turns out to be just as much fun as it is instructive.

Being pitched into the middle of ordinary people's lives lets you experience first hand the pervasive impact of the US trade embargo, and the ways in which Fair Trade initiatives have been able to circumvent it. Holiday pleasures of a more conventional kind are also included in the packed itinerary – from visiting salsa bars in Havana to trekking across mountains draped in rainforest – but it's the encounters with Cubans themselves that stand out.

One evening, we were trundled on an ox cart down 5km of bumpy track to a small wooden farm house for a typically Cuban family hog roast. Everyone from the 96-year-old patriarch, Clemente, to his great-grandchildren scampering around after the chickens, was delighted to share a meal with visitors from Canada and Europe. Afterwards, while the women were given an impromptu salsa lesson indoors, the rum and guitars appeared on the verandah, and glasses were raised in a toast to "*¡Libertad, Independencia y Comercio Justo!*" – "Freedom, Independence and Fair Trade!".

need to know

Meet the People's 15-day tour of Cuba costs £1225 ($2400), a significant proportion of which goes to the host families. For more info, see ⓦwww.skedaddle.co.uk/p2p.asp.

Tracing
15 Mandela's roots,
Eastern Cape

True to its name, South Africa's Wild Coast is one of the country's most unspoilt areas – a vast stretch of undulating hills dotted with traditional African villages, lush forest and kilometres of undeveloped beaches punctuated by rivers. Arguably the best place to taste the Wild Coast is at Bulungula Lodge, a joint enterprise between the people of Nqileni Village and seasoned traveller and development worker, Dave Martin.

Idyllically sited along the mouth of the Bulungula River, Nqileni and the lodge lie in a remote region of the former Transkei, the notionally "independent homeland" to which Xhosa-speaking black South Africans were relegated under apartheid. One consequence of South Africa's racial policies was the neglect suffered by the Wild Coast, but this also meant it escaped the intense coastal development that has ravaged many former whites-only coastal areas.

With a dearth of formal jobs, people in the Transkei still live rural lives in thatched adobe huts, growing maize, fishing and cooking on wood fires, while young lads still herd cattle, pretty much as Nelson Mandela did when he was a boy some seventy years ago. Wander around Nqileni and chances are you'll be invited into someone's house for a slug of traditional beer or you can take part in everyday business, such as mud-brick making or maize stamping.

Bulungula also gives a livelihood to members of the community, who take visitors exploring on horseback or canoeing up the Xhora River to look for malachite kingfishers, or teach them how to fish with a throw net. You can meander along the beach to watch whales and dolphins or have one of the villagers take you out on an all-day expedition to beautiful Coffee Bay. At night, the skies are so clear and the shooting stars so plentiful that, according to the lodge's owner, "if you look at the sky for half an hour without seeing one, you can stay the night for free."

need to know Accommodation at Bulungula (@www.bulungula.co.za) in four-bed huts costs R70 (£5/\$10) per person, double/twin huts go for R80 (£6/\$11.50) per person and camping costs R30 (£2/\$4.25).

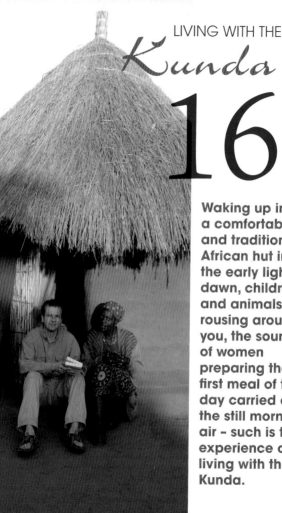

16

Waking up in a comfortable and traditional African hut in the early light of dawn, children and animals rousing around you, the sounds of women preparing the first meal of the day carried on the still morning air - such is the experience of living with the Kunda.

The villagers of Kawaza, a small hamlet on the fringes of Zambia's South Luangwa National Park, earned their livings from subsistence agriculture and working in safari lodges until they started offering tourists the chance to experience village life by spending a night or two with them. From the income this generates, the villagers – the village guides, the traditional healer I visited, and the drummers and dancers who performed a spectacular evening display for us under the moonlight – are paid. The remaining balance goes into a central fund, which the community allocates to projects such as Kawaza's village school. Six years ago the school had 327 pupils and four teachers – now there are 551 pupils and sixteen teachers.

Kawaza village consists of immaculate thatched huts or *bandas* surrounded by patchwork fields of crops. It's a happy place full of playful children, women going about their daily work and men discussing the issues of the day. You can't help but feel incredibly "grounded" in the village – maybe because somewhere in our ancient past our relatives lived in a similar way. I spent two nights there, and it's the most positive – not to mention authentic – travel experience I've had.

I spent the days in the village playing football with the kids – using a ball made out of crushed paper tied up with string – and simply sitting and talking with the locals, including an old lady from the village called Elimina Banda, who says she is happy to see whites in the village and would like to spend all day with them. "There was a time when I was scared of them," she says, "but not now."

need to know
Visiting Kawaza village (ⓦwww.kawazavillage. co.uk) costs $20 (£10) for the day, $70 (£36) overnight. Bookings can be made through Robin Pope Safaris (ⓦwww.robinpopesafaris.net), who also sponsor some of the village facilities including the school and its resources.

17 THE GREAT MEXICAN turtle arribada

It was exactly midnight when I saw my first turtle. We'd already been stumbling across the sand by torchlight for a couple of hours, following tracks up and down the beach, when one of the *patrulleros* called out of the darkness. Lumbering up the drag of white water six or seven metres from him was the unmistakeable hump of a turtle shell. I'd been wondering what it would feel like for weeks, but the sight of the pregnant female emerging from the surf after her epic journey across the entire Pacific Ocean was a moment of pure magic.

Colola Beach, on Mexico's southwest Pacific coast, is one of the last strongholds of the precariously rare Black Marine turtle. A significant proportion of the ten thousand that survive worldwide nest on its white sands each winter. Traditionally, the *arribada*, or mass nesting, in Colola would be met with knives and nets – turtle meat is a much-prized delicacy in Mexico, while the eggs are considered potent aphrodisiacs – but in recent years the local villagers have got together to reverse the decline in turtle numbers, creating in the process an alternative source of income. Supported by marine biologists from the University of Michoacán, they now run a rolling Black Turtle Camp, where volunteers from around the globe can come to help collect conservation data.

With the assistance of our *patrullero* Jesús, we followed our first turtle around the dunes for an hour until she'd found a suitable nesting site, and waited at a discreet distance while she laid her eggs. When she'd finished, we measured her and checked her shell for signs of illness or injury, while Jesús removed the clutch to a secret spot further into the dunes, beyond the reach of poachers.

Forty-five days later, those same eggs would hatch, and other volunteers would be there to give the hatchlings a helping hand, transporting them in a bucket to the surf, where they'd begin their long swim to their nesting grounds on the other side of the Pacific.

need to know

For more info, see Ⓦwww. responsibletravel.com. The two-week trip costs £550/$1000, excluding flights. The prime turtle nesting season lasts from mid-November to early December.

Over two million people descend on the French Mediterranean island of Corsica each year, the vast majority of them to laze on its legendary turquoise and white-sand coast. Aided by the antics of second-home-bombing, nationalist paramilitaries, the French Government has enforced its strict environmental laws to good effect. But even so, the pressure on the beaches in peak season is definitely à la limite. Which is why increasing numbers of savvy visitors are eschewing the joys of la plage for the equally spectacular – but much less frequented – montagne.

Depopulated by two world wars, Corsica's scattered stone villages sit quietly on hillsides swathed in decaying chestnut and olive orchards, their slender Baroque belfries pointing skywards to high, cloud-swept ridges of grey granite. Following an ancient network of trails, the regional national park has established eleven long-distance walking itineraries. Each is divided into manageable five- to seven-hour stages, or étapes. In the course of any one of them you might find yourself scaling 1000-metre passes, crossing noisy waterfalls, dipping in deep, green pools, or skirting remote sea coves overshadowed by cliffs of blood-red porphyry.

With the exception of the GR20 (Corsica's most physically demanding mountain route, where trekkers camp or sleep in refuges at altitude), accommodation comes in the form of simple gîtes d'étapes, or hikers' hostels, where you can eat wholesome local cooking and recover from the day's travails enjoying the views from a terrasse panoramique. Staying in gîtes not only frees you from having to carry a tent, but also ensures what little you spend on your holiday goes straight into your Corsican hosts' pockets.

Moreover, as each of Corsica's trails begins and ends a stone's throw from the coast, you can recover from the walk by joining the masses on the island's amazingly white beaches.

need to know

Corsica's trekking network offers routes lasting from two to fourteen days, and there's plenty of scope for linking them together to form longer walks. Full details of all accommodation available along the way is listed in the Rough Guide to Corsica.

TREKKING
in Corsica
18

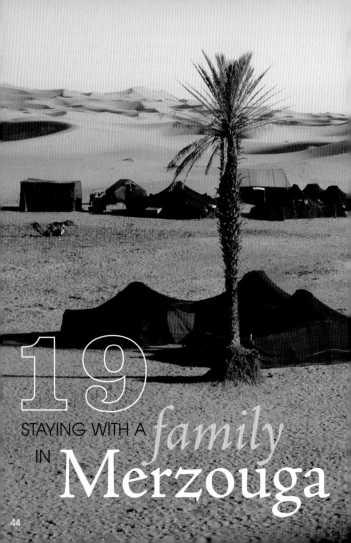

19

STAILING WITH A *family*
IN
Merzouga

Waking up in a nomad's black-wool tent, surrounded by mile upon mile of ochre-coloured sand dunes, the first thing that struck me was the silence: a deep, muffled nothing. The second was the cold. Even beneath a stack of blankets, it was chilly enough to numb the end of my nose. Only after three glasses of mint tea by the fireside were my fingers warm enough to tackle the zip on my puffer jacket and help saddle up the camels for the day's trek.

Despite the chilly mornings, January is the best month to visit southern Morocco's Erg Chebbi dunes. The skies are big and blue, the horizons crisp and, best of all, the hordes who descend here later in the year blissfully absent. Back at our guesthouse, *Chez Tihri*, at the end of our morning's ride, we could enjoy the wondrous spectacle of the sand hills in peace and quiet.

Chez Tihri is a rarity in a corner of the country notorious for its highly commoditized versions of the desert and its people: an auberge run by a Tamasheq-speaking Amazigh (Touareg) where you actually feel a genuine sense of place. Built in old-school kasbah style, its crenellated pisé walls, adorned with bold geometric patterns in patriotic reds and greens, shelter a warren of cosy rooms, each decorated with rugs, pottery and lanterns, and interconnected by dark, earthy corridors.

As well as being a congenial host, Omar Tihri, dressed in imposing white turban and flowing robe, is a passionate advocate for Amazigh traditions and culture and living proof that tourism can be a force for good in this region. A slice of the profits from *Chez Tihri* go towards funding a women's weaving co-op, in addition to a small school where Tamasheq-speaking children, who are poorly catered for by the mainstream state education in the area, can learn French and Arabic.

need to know

Auberge Chez Tihri (Ⓦwww.tuaregexpeditions.com) lies 2km north of Merzouga; turn left at the signboard on the main road and follow the piste as far as the dunes. Rates start at £15/$27 per night half board for two. Camel treks can be organized through the auberge from £13.50/$25.50 per night.

20 Beating the drought in the Thar, Rajasthan

"People in the villages use only around fifteen litres of water for their daily bath, but a western shower uses two or three times that,"

explains our host, Ramesh, to a middle-aged Swiss lady who's confused by the presence of a large plastic bucket and mug in her bathroom. He hands her a copy of the lodge's Advice to Visitors on which the process of how Rajasthanis wash is elucidated, step-by-step: "1. They first soak themselves, taking water from the bucket with the mug; 2. Then they apply soap; 3. Finally, they rinse themselves." The Swiss lady seems delighted, and skips off to enjoy a water-saving sluice-over.

Saving water, as you soon find out, is a way of life in Shekhawati, a drought-prone region on the fringes of Rajasthan's great Thar desert. Average rainfall here has dropped over the past decade to less than 300mm per year – a quarter of the Indian norm. Ensuring visitors waste as little as possible, as well as efficiently harvesting what does fall in the annual monsoons, are thus high priorities at Ramesh Jangid's self-styled "eco-hotel", Apani Dhani.

Fusing traditional Rajasthani construction methods with modern renewable-energy technology, Ramesh created his small campus of baked-mud and thatch roundel "huts" for visitors to use as a homely base from which to explore the surrounding region. Solar panels provide hot water and lighting in the huts, the meals served under cascades of bougainvillea in the central courtyard are cooked with organic produce from the garden, using biogas. And any waste – from potato peelings to the little dry-leaf plates you eat off – is composted or recycled.

In the village of Shekhawati, as in others, camels can still be seen hauling water from deep pits in the sand – a spectacle that must be much harder to enjoy after a water-squandering shower than a soak in Ramesh's old-fashioned bucket bath.

need to know

Rooms at **Apani Dhani** cost around Rs1000 (£11.75/\$22.20) per night. Cultural excursions around Shekhawati – by camel, cart, or jeep – can be arranged on arrival. Prices range from Rs1500 to 2000 (£17.50–23.50/\$33.30–44.40) per day for up to four people. Ⓦwww.apanidhani.com.

21

REVEL *in eco luxury*
at Morgan's Rock

The largest area of virgin rainforest north of the Amazon, endless miles of pristine coastline, 76 national parks brimming with wildlife, six active volcanoes – Nicaragua is an eco-tourist's fantasy. After decades of political turbulence, the largest country in Central America is set to become the buzz word for adventurous travellers with a conscience – like Costa Rica before the swarm.

Leading the way in terms of environmentally friendly accommodation is the country's first five-star resort, Morgan's Rock Hacienda and Ecolodge. The hacienda's fifteen chalets are built like stupendous treehouses, with open sides offering gorgeous views onto a private beach, where giant leatherback turtles lay their eggs; wake in the night to witness hundreds of flapping babies (August to January). Simple furniture is handmade by regional artisans, the friendly staff are locals and the open-air showers are heated by solar panels.

This is a hotel that takes the eco part of its billing incredibly seriously. Behind the scenes, *Morgan's* is a clean dream of organic living. The owners of the hacienda have planted almost 1.5 million trees and have set aside 800 hectares of primary forest for conservation – home to spider monkeys, armadillos and sloths, as well as dozens of exotic birds, and brought alive on awesome wildlife tours by trained biologists. Endangered animal species are being reintroduced, whilst existing animals are protected from hunters. Then there is the restaurant, which offers some of the freshest, purest food you will ever taste – including organic algae-fed shrimp, cheese made from the hacienda's cows, and sweet homemade rum.

Luxurious ethical travel doesn't come better than this. Enjoy moonlit walks on the beach or wallow in the salt-water pool, happy in the knowledge that what's good for you is also good for the planet. It's back-to-nature bliss.

need to know

Morgan's Rock is situated to the north of San Juan del Sur, a two-hour drive from Granada. Rates range from $158 to 302 per person per night and include three daily meals, local beverages and two daily tours. ⓦwww. morgansrock.com.

49

VOLUNTEERING

in Cambodia

with VSO

Thirty years after Pol Pot's notorious Khmer Rouge, VSO (Voluntary Service Overseas) now runs one of its largest country programmes in Cambodia, with ninety volunteers working to improve health and education systems and help build secure livelihoods. I joined their programme in Kampong Cham, working with an NGO to help improve local school curriculum through creative techniques such as art therapy and dance. The aim is to encourage children to express themselves and in time challenge the legacy of the Khmer Rouge, who left behind them a culture of fear and conformity.

Part of my role in schools was encouraging communication between boys and girls. Marital breakdown and domestic violence are common and high school drop-out rates for girls especially are high; tackling this together with local leadership seemed to me a really tangible benefit of volunteering. We would mix boys and girls in the classroom so they could talk to each other more freely, and then introduce art or dance activities where they would role-play everyday life and talk about what they had learned.

Over the year, I was inundated with invitations to people's homes and was even befriended by Buddhist monks keen to get me on board as a catalyst for reopening a street children's centre. I was eager to learn and feel at home myself and this sharing process affected me as much as my local counterparts, challenging the taboos of my own culture in return.

Towards the end of the placement my Khmer became pretty fluent, giving me an insight into local life that I would have missed otherwise. I loved listening to conversations about me on the bus – "Where is she from?", "Why is she on her own?", "I think I've seen her around on her bicycle", and my personal favourite, "Doesn't she have a nice nose?" – and I'd pipe up half way through the journey speaking my Khmer and the whole bus would fall about laughing.

need to know

VSO is an international development agency operating in over thirty countries. Volunteers aged 18 to 75 are placed according to their skills and experience in projects ranging from one month to two years. All placements work together with local people to combat poverty and disadvantage. For more information visit ⓦwww.vso.org.uk.

LEARNING TO
survive
in deepest Dorset

It looked like something Bilbo Baggins might have kept his compost in. But for me, and the couple of other bushcraft students, the forest pod proved a very cosy shelter indeed. We'd spent most of the previous afternoon learning how to build it from deadwood gathered off the floor of our coppice in Dorset. Clad in leafy branches of beech and chestnut, with a low opening as an entrance, it must have been pretty close to what our ancestors would have put together on hunting trips thousands of years ago.

23

Reviving lost survival techniques as a means to getting closer to nature is very much the underlying goal of Bushcraft Week. Our instructor, Andy "Woody" Wood, is an ex-military man who has spent years living, travelling and hunting with indigenous people, from the polar ice cap to the Kalahari, soaking up their wilderness skills and, in the process, re-kindling in himself a more intimate relationship with his native British environment.

Under Woody's expert guidance we learn the correct way to lay fires and how to use naturally flammable fungus to light them; how to dig out an earth oven to cook in; and select wood that becomes hot coals instead of tinder when lit. For implements, we're taught Scandinavian carving methods and shown ways to turn brass picture framing wire into lethal rabbit snares. Thankfully, these are never laid, but one day we're given a sack of dead bunnies to skin, dress and cook, along with pot herbs we gather from the forest.

After a week amid the greenery, I emerge a more contented creature than I was before, smelling strongly of woodsmoke and roast rabbit but seeing the world – or, at least, the bits of it covered in trees instead of tarmac – in an altogether different light. And you never know: in these times of melting icebergs and rising water levels, they might just come in useful one day.

need to know

For more info, see Ⓦwww.bushcraftexpeditions.com. The week-long course costs £480 ($905). Woody also runs bushcraft courses in Norway, Borneo, Thailand and Namibia.

It's 5am; dawn's chorus of mellifluous birds propel me into consciousness even before the sun can wrap its (not so temperate) fingers around the eucalypts. The air, fresh with lemon and lime, wafts through the mosquito-net mesh that passes for the windows of my tin shack. Perfect timing – I can just about fit in a spot of breakfast before work.

Thus begins a typical day down on Wilderness Organic Farm, 50km north of Katherine in Australia's Outback, Northern Territory. Part of WWOOF (World-Wide Opportunities on Organic Farms), which was set up by Sue Coppard in 1971 and now has national organizations in 24 countries, Wilderness takes in willing workers for anything from a week to several months, providing them with a bed for the night and three meals a day (organic, of course) in exchange for five hours of daily work – anything from planting capsicum and tomato seedlings, mulching lemon plants and harvesting mangoes to painting farm buildings, cooking and baking. Anything, basically, that might need doing in the daily life of a sub-tropical, Outback agricultural establishment. And by "smoko", an archaic Aussie term for mid-morning tea break, you'll be glad you got the hard graft out of the way during the cooler part of the day as temperatures soar to 40°C by 11am.

There's certainly never a dull moment when you're working and living with locals, migrant workers and backpackers from all over the world, swapping stories (and a few toasted marshmallows) around the campfire. Besides, work will be nothing but a distant memory by the time you've cooled off in the Edith River after lunch, eaten barbecued kangaroo with homebrewed mango wine for dinner, and been lulled to sleep by a symphony of cicadas under a star-puckered black canvas at night.

need to know

For a full list of member countries, check out WWOOF's wesbite Ⓦwww.wwoof.org. As a member (£15 per year in the UK – see website for other countries) you'll have access to contact details for a wide variety of organic farms all over the world.

GOING
organic
in the
Northern
Territory

24

"There's certainly never a dull moment when you're working and living with locals, migrant workers and backpackers from all over the world, swapping stories (and a few toasted marshmallows) around the campfire."

25

COUNTING FISH
in the Philippines

Emperors, damsels, parrots and snappers
– they were all down there in the Sulu Sea off the Philippine island of Palawan. I scribbled their names on an underwater slate as we drifted over the reef, air bubbles rising twenty metres to the humid surface.

It was my second week of identifying fish – their features now familiar after a week of lectures and tests on reef ecology – on an expedition run by Coral Cay Conservation (CCC); others in my survey team were noting corals, sponges and invertebrates. The hump-headed shape of a Napoleon Wrasse, almost two metres long and most often found on dinner plates in the Far East, had me writing in large capitals. I tugged on the survey rope to alert the others, just in time to see it disappear among the rocks below.

As we began our ascent, we heard the familiar metallic "plink" of dynamite fishing in the distance, and it wasn't too difficult to picture the damsels, parrots and snappers being blasted out of their hiding places, to float – dazed and injured – into the waiting nets above.

Back at base – an almost clichéd tropical island idyll – we entered our data into special forms used to provide a picture of the reef's diversity and to create sustainable development plans for local communities. As dusk fell and gas lamps were lit, we began our nightly ritual, heading down to the beach to rate the sunset. Walking back along the sandy path, iguanas rustling either side, I wondered whether Napoleon would still be there tomorrow.

need to know

CCC sends teams of volunteers to survey some of the world's most endangered coral reefs and rainforests, with two-week – and longer – expeditions in Fiji, Tobago, the Philippines and Papua New Guinea. Volunteers require no scientific background and are trained on-site in marine or terrestrial ecology and survey techniques. For more information, visit Ⓦwww.coralcay.org.

Ultimate
experiences
Ethical
Travel
miscellany

1 Travel and climate change

There's no getting away from it. Regardless of how ethical your holiday might be, if you've had to travel to get there you'll have inflicted some damage on the environment.

Emissions of greenhouse gases from trains, planes and automobiles are major contributors to climate change. Air travel, however, is the most damaging of all – principally because it enables us to travel much greater distances than we might otherwise. An accurate comparison would have to take into account vehicle types and occupancy levels, but on average, airplanes discharge 25 percent more carbon dioxide into the atmosphere, per head per mile, than cars. A return flight for two between New York and London, for example, generates over 3 tonnes of CO_2 – more than the output from the average family home in a year, or the equivalent of driving 10,000 miles.

"The saying 'getting there is half the fun' became obsolete with the advent of commercial airlines."

Henry J Tillman

2 Five ways to cut your carbon footprint

- Travel less and stay longer.
- Travel by a cleaner means – eg trains instead of planes, bicycles instead of cars.
- Offset your carbon emissions (see opposite).
- Use local transport instead of hire cars.
- Explore holiday opportunities in your own country.

3 Climate neutral travel

You can neutralize the effect of your travel on climate change by "offsetting" its carbon output – ie paying an organization to reduce CO_2 in the atmosphere by the same amount as your travel will add. Rough Guides have teamed up with the organization Climate Care, who – at the click of a mouse – will calculate your carbon use and then invest on your behalf in a range of carbon-reducing projects, such as forest restoration (planting trees to absorb CO_2) or schemes to promote energy efficient products. For more, go to: Ⓦ www.roughguides.com/climatechange.

4 Mass tourism

No one can know for sure how many journeys are made on our planet in any given year, but the World Tourism Organization keeps tabs on the number of leisure trips worldwide: more than 800 million in 2005. Generating around US$705 billion (£379 billion) annually, tourism provides around 200 million jobs and accounts for more than 10 percent of the world's total GDP. And, in spite of terrorist attacks, bird flu and tsunamis, the sector is growing year on year at record-breaking rates, especially in developing countries such as Thailand, India, Costa Rica and Vietnam. By 2020, the number of "non-essential" international trips is expected to top 1.6 billion.

5 Five most popular holiday destinations

France	75.5 million visitors per year
USA	51 million visitors per year
Spain	48.2 million visitors per year
Italy	41.2 million visitors per year
China	31.2 million visitors per year

6 The tourist: friend or foe?

Tourism has the potential to be an enormously positive force for both visitors and hosts. It can be a particular boon in poorer countries, where other sources of income might not exist, creating employment, promoting gender equality and protecting the natural environment.

But the benefits are not always ideally balanced. The past fifty years have thrown up ample proof of what mass tourism can do to fragile environments, economies and cultures if it's insensitively managed. Moreover, the problems are most likely to run out of control in precisely those parts of the world that stand to gain most from extra tourist dollars.

"He who would travel happily must travel light."

Antoine de Saint-Exupéry, aviator and writer

7 Five examples of negative impact

Southeastern Spain The demands of hundreds of thousands of high-rise hotels and swimming pools in this drought-prone region has caused a dramatic drop in ground water levels; seawater in Benidorm has started to poison surrounding farmland. Mallorca, in the Balearics, has seen its water table plunge 90m in two decades.

The Alps Few corners of Europe's highest mountain range have escaped the blights of a booming winter sports industry: soil erosion, deforestation, landscaping, unsightly pylons and ski lifts.

Goa, India Mechanized trawler fishing to supply the tourist market in this former Portuguese colony has virtually wiped out local in-shore fishing, depriving poorer coastal villages of their traditional livelihoods.

The Dominican Republic The largest all-inclusive long-haul destination in the world, with 50,000 rooms – yet little of the revenue reaches ordinary Dominicans, ninety percent of whom live below the poverty line.

Cruise ship pollution Ocean liners are notorious polluters of the seas. In one week, your average cruise ship will illegally dump into the waves one million gallons of grey water (from sinks, laundries and galleys), 210,000 gallons of sewerage and fifty tonnes of garbage, not to mention vast amounts of bilge water and toxic waste.

8 Definitions . . .

"Responsible", "ethical", "sustainable" and "alternative" tourism are tags whose meanings are much debated by specialists, but for the purposes of this book, they're virtually interchangeable, denoting a kind of holiday experience which seeks to minimize its impact on the environment while maximizing benefits for local people. From the mixed bag we've picked out, you'll appreciate how flexible these definitions can be.

9 Greenwashing

Just like organic coffee or fair-trade bananas, responsible holidays tend to cost a fraction more than less ethical alternatives. Unfortunately, unscrupulous operators may seek to cash in on this perceived green premium by simply dressing up their business as more environmentally friendly or beneficial to locals than it really is – a process known as "greenwashing". This may be as innocuous as little notices in a boutique hotel telling you your towels are washed in biodegradable laundry powder (while it dumps untreated sewerage in the river). Or it might involve more sinister developments which, while calling themselves "green", are in fact damaging biodiversity or harming the livelihoods of local communities.

"If tour operators do not have an ethical code and are not providing information to tourists on the benefits they bring to people in the destinations, it is doubtful they know themselves what impact they are having."

Graham Gordon, Tearfund (anti-poverty pressure group)

10 Volunteering: five questions

Volunteering abroad can be a highly rewarding experience, both for the volunteers and for the communities benefiting from their time and skills. However, this sector is particularly rife with money-making schemes masquerading as development projects. Here are five questions to help sort the true green wheat from the paler green chaff:

- Was the project simply created to sell holidays?
- Is the project run in partnership with local people?
- Will you be working alongside local people to transfer skills?
- What proportion of the overall profits are returned to the local community?
- Could I see some independent research on the results of the project?

11 Leakage

All too often, the lion's share of the money spent on a holiday goes not to people in the area you travel to, but to middlemen. The UK-based organization Tourism Concern (www.tourismconcern.org.uk) has highlighted a prime example of such "leakage": a package safari holiday in Kenya. Out of every pound spent by the customer, 40p typically gets soaked up by the airline, 23p by the hotel chain, 20p by the travel agent and 8p by the safari company. Not a penny ends up in the pockets of the local Maasai, the traditional inhabitants of the lands where the safaris are run. The Kenyan government recoups 9p in the pound as taxes, but 15 percent of that dribbles away on debt repayment.

The main beneficiaries of "leakage" are the large package tour operators who nowadays control most of the tourism industry. In the UK, their grip is all but absolute; just four firms hold sway over 80 percent of the market. And because their empires include not just travel agents, but also airlines and often whole hotels, these big hitters are the main reason so little of the money from tourism stays in host countries.

 # Community tourism

Community tourism initiatives are holiday initiatives run by, and primarily for the benefit of, local people rather than outside operators. Unlike most mainstream package tours, the bulk of the money reaches those who live in the area you're visiting. Homestays in marginal communities, such as those in Kumaon (see p.10–11), Anapia (see p.32–33) and Kawaza (see p.38–39), are good examples. By making interactions between visitors and hosts more equitable, grassroots holidays also render the whole experience a more positive one for both parties.

 # Water

All that extra water required by hotels for cooking, laundry, showers, swimming pools and keeping lawns green can place an immense burden on local supplies, leading to shortages. The biggest water guzzlers of all, though, are golf courses. It has been estimated that a typical 18-hole course drinks up around one million litres per day.

"All journeys have secret destinations of which the traveller is unaware."

Martin Buber, philosopher, translator and educator

 # Coral reefs

Poorly managed tourism is a major contributing factor in the worldwide degeneration of coral reefs. Snorkelling, scuba diving and yacht anchors may inflict direct physical damage, but construction in coastal areas causes sediment to drain into the sea and block light, leading to so-called "coral bleaching". Sewerage from boats and hotels also promotes the growth of algae, which can suffocate reefs.

On the other hand, tourism can play a positive role in protecting coral, funding marine parks and important survey work. One such example is featured on p.56–57.

 Displacement

The displacement of local people to make way for resorts or conservation areas is a major concern in some developing countries. In India and Africa, for example, whole settlements have been abandoned to make way for wildlife reserves, generating resentment among villagers – and intensifying poaching of the very animals the parks were set up to protect.

All-in beach resorts are other prime offenders, frequently excluding locals from traditional fishing, hunting or gathering grounds in order to sanitize the sands for their visitors. However, not all beach and wildlife holidays need exclude local participation, as several examples in this book show (see p.14–15 and p.24–25).

16 Erosion of traditional cultures

When tourist dollars collide with traditional economies, old ways of life are often swept aside. But when local people have a say in the way tourism is run on their land, and receive a just share of the rewards, visitors can definitely be a force for good, helping to preserve respect for what, to younger generations, may seem out-moded or irrelevant customs. Outside interest in minority or indigenous communities can also raise their international profile, helping to protect them from land-, log- or water-grabbing governments. Not least of all, tourism may provide income in marginal areas where no other source of cash is available, or where traditional means of making money have been outlawed.

17 Cultural sensitivity

As well as enriching your travels, a bit of research into local culture will lessen the risk of causing offence. While your well-meaning eco-dollars will always be welcome, your choice of beach-wear may not. Here are some things to look out for, particularly outside of Europe, North America and Australasia:

- **Religion** Religion still plays a major part in most people's lives around the world and respect should be paid accordingly: take care not mock or insult religious beliefs or figures; when visiting religious monuments, always check for restrictions regarding clothing, use of cameras, etc.
- **Clothing** Clothing, or lack of it, is the thing that's most likely to cause offence. Check locally, but modest clothing is almost certainly required in any public building or space. Baring your flesh on beaches and nude bathing is considered extremely unpalatable in many countries.
- **Public behaviour** Public displays of physical affection, anger and drunkenness are very much Western practices and should be avoided.
- **Social conventions** In Japan, it is considered rude to blow your nose; in Thailand, you should never touch another person's head; in Islamic countries, always ensure you're not pointing the soles of your feet at anyone. Do your research before you go and avoid embarrassment.
- **Language** Attempting to speak at least a few words of the local lingo can only be viewed positively by your hosts.

"When you travel, remember that a foreign country is not designed to make you comfortable. It is designed to make its own people comfortable."

Clifton Fadiman, intellectual and broadcaster

18 Ethical packing

Ethical travel is all very well, but if you're travelling the world in crocodile shoes, a fur hat and a sweatshop sweater, your credentials will be shaky to say the least. To stay abreast of labour developments, check out ⓦwww.cleanclothes.org and ⓦwww.sweatshopwatch.org. Seek out items bearing the Fairtrade mark and avoid clothing made in Burma – purchases help bolster an extremely oppressive regime. While no retailer is perfect, ⓦwww.clothworks.co.uk, ⓦwww.greenfibres.com, ⓦwww.naturalcollection.com and ⓦwww.patagonia.com are all worth a look.

19 Five award and certification schemes

- **First Choice Responsible Travel Awards** The largest scheme of its kind in the world, now in its fourth year, the Awards are a collaboration between online travel agent responsibletravel.com, which organizes them; UK media partners *The Times* and *Geographical Magazine;* supporters Conservation International; and The World Travel Market, which hosts the presentation event. The central tenet of the Awards is that all types of tourism – from niche to mainstream – can and should be operated in a way that respects and benefits destinations and local people. ⓦwww.responsibletravel.com.

- **World Legacy Awards** Overseen by *National Geographic Traveler* magazine and Conservation International, this programme honours "businesses, organizations and places that have made a significant contribution to promoting the principles of sustainable tourism". ⓦwww.wlaward.org.

- **Green Globe** Certification scheme for the global tourism industry, founded by a consortium of major hotel chains, airlines and tour operators. ⓦwww.greenglobe.org.

- **British Airways Tourism For Tomorrow Awards** Since 1992 BA have sponsored this award scheme, which sets out to "recognise and promote the world's leading examples of best practice in responsible tourism development". ⓦwww.tourismfortomorrow.com.

- **EU Eco-label** The Flower Logo rewards any form of tourist accommodation – whether "Mediterranean hotel chain, or a city hotel palace, a mountain hut, a B&B or a farm house" – that's made an outstanding effort to be environmentally friendly. ⓦwww.eco-label-tourism.com.

"Sentiment without action is the ruin of the soul."

Edward Abbey, www.ResponsibleTravel.com

20 DIY responsible holidays

One watertight way to ensure nearly all of what you spend in a foreign country stays there, benefiting the local economy rather than outside agents, is to organize the holiday yourself. A good guidebook will help you track down those minimum impact hotels, eco-lodges, homestays and community-based tourism projects. Travelling independently rather than on an organized tour, you're also more likely to depend on local transport, radically lessening your carbon footprint. Again, your trusty guidebook should show you the way.

21 Hotels

Gone are the days when a "green" holiday meant having to rough it in a boggy camping field. Here are five high-end places to stay where luxury doesn't cost the earth:

- **Green Hotel**, Mysore, India ⓦwww.cardaid.co.uk/greenhotel. Former royal palace restored as a model of sustainable development, with all profits going to charitable and environmental projects in the region.

- **Nihiwatu**, Indonesia ⓦwww.nihiwatu.com. This award-winning, chic little hideaway sits on a remote island in Indonesia's southeastern chain. It's amazingly beautiful, and makes a positive contribution to the lives of local minority people.

- **Daintree EcoLodge & Spa**, Australia ⓦwww.daintree-ecolodge.com.au. Unique and award-winning tree-house-style resort on Australia's Great Barrier Reef.

- **Kicheche Mara Camp**, Kenya ⓦwww.kicheche.com. Traditional bush camp in the heart of Kenya's Maasai Mara. The camp impinges so little on the wildlife that animals wander through the grounds unperturbed.

- **Islas Secas**, Panama ⓦwww.islassecas.com. Entirely solar powered luxury resort set amid sixteen secluded tropical islands.

22 Guilt-free trips: five do's and don'ts

▶▶ Do . . .

… neutralize your carbon footprint through a website such as ⓦwww.climatecare.org.

… book your flight through an ethical travel agent such as North South Travel (ⓦwww.northsouthtravel.co.uk). If you're travelling on a package, aim for an operator with an accredited responsible tourism policy.

… use public transport instead of hire cars to get around.

… choose local services, accommodation and goods rather than imported or foreign-owned ones.

… stay somewhere that has a strict, effective environmental policy, recycles its waste and minimizes water use.

▶▶ Don't . . .

… opt for an all-inclusive holiday.

… fly if it's viable to get there by rail.

… buy bottled water; filter or chlorinate tap water to cut down on non-biodegradable plastic waste.

… buy souvenirs made from wild animal parts or rare hardwoods.

… disregard local norms, especially dress codes – even on the beach.

"I dislike feeling at home when I am abroad."

George Bernard Shaw

23 Responsible tourism on the rise

"Eco-", "Environmental" or "Responsible" tourism is the fastest growing sector in the industry, with growth rates of 10 percent to 30 percent per year – or around one in five tourists worldwide.

24 Five recommended books

The Ethical Travel Guide Polly Pattullo with Orely Minelli (2006, Earthscan/Tourism Concern)

The Rough Guide to Ethical Living Duncan Clark (2006, Rough Guides)

The Rough Guide to Climate Change Robert Henson (2006, Rough Guides)

Ethical Tourism: Who Benefits? Institute of Ideas (2002, Hodder Arnold H&S)

Green Places to Stay edited by Richard Hammond (2006, Alastair Sawday Publishing)

25 Human rights

Opinion is divided over whether or not tourists should boycott countries with poor human rights records. Advocates of embargoes claim that merely by setting foot in states such as Burma or the Maldives, where tourism infrastructures have allegedly been built using forced labour and where any dissent from official policy is brutally suppressed, you're both condoning the oppression and contributing financially to the regime. Opponents, on the other hand, insist boycotts are ineffective and only aggravate poverty on the ground; better, they say, to manage the dilemma by channeling visitors through privately owned and grass roots businesses, with no connection to the government.

Wherever you travel, if you're in any doubt about the human rights credentials of your host government, check the situation out with your agent. Another source of information is the campaign group Tourism Concern (Ⓦwww.tourismconcern.org.uk), which collects histories of human rights abuses perpetrated by governments of countries with tourism interests. Amnesty International's website (Ⓦwww.amnesty.org) also gives details of countries accused of human rights abuses.

Ultimate
experiences
Ethical
Travel
small print

ROUGH GUIDES – don't just travel

We hope you've been inspired by the experiences in this book. There are 24 other books in the 25 Ultimate Experiences series, each conceived to whet your appetite for travel and for everything the world has to offer. As well as covering the globe, the 25s series also includes books on **Journeys, World Food, Adventure Travel, Places to Stay, Wildlife Adventures** and **Wonders of the World**.

When you start planning your trip, Rough Guides' new-look guides, maps and phrasebooks are the ultimate companions. For 25 years we've been refining what makes a good guidebook and we now include more colour photos and more information – on average 50% more pages – than any of our competitors. Just look for the sky-blue spines.

Rough Guides don't just travel – we also believe in getting the most out of life without a passport. Since the publication of the bestselling Rough Guides to **The Internet** and **World Music**, we've brought out a wide range of lively and authoritative guides on everything from **Climate Change** to **Hip-Hop**, from **MySpace** to **Film Noir** and from **The Brain** to **The Rolling Stones**.

Publishing information

Rough Guide 25 Ultimate experiences
Ethical Travel Published May 2007 by Rough
Guides Ltd, 80 Strand, London WC2R 0RL
345 Hudson St, 4th Floor,
New York, NY 10014, USA
14 Local Shopping Centre, Panchsheel Park,
New Delhi 110017, India
Distributed by the Penguin Group
Penguin Books Ltd,
80 Strand, London WC2R 0RL
Penguin Group (USA)
375 Hudson Street, NY 10014, USA
Penguin Group (Australia)
250 Camberwell Road, Camberwell,
Victoria 3124, Australia
Penguin Books Canada Ltd,
10 Alcorn Avenue, Toronto, Ontario,
Canada M4V 1E4
Penguin Group (NZ)
67 Apollo Drive, Mairangi Bay, Auckland 1310,
New Zealand

Printed in China
© Rough Guides 2007
No part of this book may be reproduced in
any form without permission from the publisher
except for the quotation of brief passages in
reviews.
80pp
A catalogue record for this book is available
from the British Library
ISBN: 978-1-84353-830-1
The publishers and authors have done their
best to ensure the accuracy and currency of
all the information in Rough Guide 25 Ultimate
experiences Ethical Travel, however, they can
accept no responsibility for any loss, injury, or
inconvenience sustained by any traveller as
a result of information or advice contained in
the guide.

1   3   5   7   9   8   6   4   2

Rough Guide credits

Editors: Keith Drew, Joanna Kirby
Design & picture research: Diana Jarvis
Cartography: Katie Lloyd-Jones,
Maxine Repath

Cover design: Diana Jarvis, Chloë Roberts
Production: Aimee Hampson, Katherine Owers
Proofreaders: Megan McIntyre, Sarah Eno

The authors

Dave Abram (Experiences 1, 2, 7, 8, 10, 13, 14, 17, 18, 19, 20 and 23) is author of the *Rough Guide to Goa* and the *Rough Guide to Corsica*, and co-author of the *Rough Guide to India*.

Harriet Mills (Experience 3) is a member and volunteer for the Dorset Wildlife Trust.

Richard Trillo (Experience 4) is author of the *Rough Guide to Kenya*.

Keith Drew (Experience 5) is a Senior Editor at Rough Guides and a freelance travel journalist.

Matthew Teller (Experiences 6 and 11) is author of the *Rough Guide to Jordan*.

Polly Thomas (Experience 9) is co-author of the *Rough Guide to Jamaica*.

Mark Ellingham (Experience 12) took his family to Costa Rica in 2006.

Tony Pinchuk (Experience 15) is co-author of the *Rough Guide to South Africa* and the *Rough Guide to Cape Town & the Garden Route*.

Justin Francis (Experience 16) co-founded responsibletravel.com, an online travel agent specializing in holidays that maximize the positive impact of tourism and minimize the negative.

Daisy Finer (Experience 21). A seasoned traveller and travel writer, Daisy seeks out sustainable tourism options wherever possible.

Rob Coates (Experience 22), on behalf of Hannah Snowden. Rob is a Programme Officer at VSO.

Diana Jarvis (Experience 24) is an organic food enthusiast and plans to have an organic smallholding of her own one day.

Andy Turner (Experience 25). An experienced and enthusiastic scuba diver, Andy has applied his aquatic skills to marine life conservation in both the Philippines and Fiji.

Picture credits

ROUGH GUIDES

New Zealand

Budapest

ROUGH GUIDES

Thailand

ROUGH GUIDES

Greece

ROUGH GUIDES

Punk

ROUGH GUIDES

Italy

ROUGH GUIDES

India

Over 70 reference books and hundreds of travel
guides, maps & phrasebooks that cover the worl

BROADEN YOUR HORIZONS

www.roughguides.com

Index